Earthlight

Earthlight

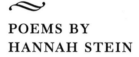

POEMS BY
HANNAH STEIN

La Questa PRESS

Earthlight
Copyright © 2000 Hannah Stein
All rights reserved

La Questa Press
211 La Questa Way
Woodside, California 94062

www.laquestapress.com

Cover and text design by Kajun Design

Cover art, "Getting From Here to There," mixed media
collage/canvas, © 1999 by Barbara K. Schwartz, courtesy of
Viridian Artists Inc. NYC and Vita Sorrell.

ISBN 0-9644348-3-0
Library of Congress Catalog Card Number: 99-73386

For Sherman—always

and with gratitude to my family, my friends, and my teachers, to whom I and this book owe so much.

ACKNOWLEDGMENTS

American Literary Review: "Seeing Double"
The American Voice: "Twin"
Americas Review: "At the End of the Century"
The Antioch Review: "The Turning" Copyright (c) 1988 by the Antioch
  Review, Inc. First appeared in *The Antioch Review*, Vol. 46, No. 3
  (Summer 1988). Reprinted by permission of the editors.
Beloit Poetry Journal: "The Road to Giverny," "Lapsed Agnostic"
California Quarterly: "Reading the Reflections Backward," "Messenger,"
  "The Waterfall"
Chariton Review: "Madame Monet in the Garden"
Cumberland Poetry Review: "Fragile"
Kayak: "Hunger Strike" (reprinted in *Americas Review*)
The Literary Review: "About Time"
Lullwater Review: "This Time, This Place"
MSS: "The Ladder"
Passages North: "Walking Up the Hill"
Poetry Flash: "It Looks Like Up," "Waiting for the Cranes"
Poetry Northwest: "Grace," "The Country of Hope," "Improvisation"
Poetry Now: "Among Treetops"
Prairie Schooner: "The Distance to the Ocean," "Lighthouse at Point
  Reyes," "Winter in Fox-Light," "A View of the Lagoon"
Slant: "899 Montgomery Street"
Solo: "All but the Blackberries Themselves"
The Tule Review: "A Gap in the Dark"
Windhorse Review: "Progress Report"
The Yale Review: "Anniversary: *after Chagall*"

Several of these poems are included in a chapbook, *Schools of Flying
Fish*, published by State Street Press. "The Turning" and "Walking Up the
Hill" were republished in the *Anthology of Magazine Verse & Yearbook of
American Poetry* and "Fragile" was republished in *The State Street
Reader.* "The Ladder" first appeared in the *National Poetry Competition
Winners Anthology* and "Among Treetops" first appeared in *Penelope
Flowers.*

Earthlight

CONTENTS

I

II

III

I

And the heart does not die when one thinks it should,
we smile, there is tea and bread on the table.

— *Czeslaw Milosz, "Elegy for N.N."*

TWIN

...we still love life,...we still hope, hope about everything.
—*Anne Frank*

How could you have died: I
would have sensed it.
Without having seen you
I know you are the one
who suffered, who was made to touch
the dead. Your mouth was filled
with stones. It was you who tore
giving birth, I who only knew
something was tearing. We have caught
the same fevers at the same
moment: we wait to become real
to one another.

They would have taken me as I sat
on a stone bench in a desolate yard
or walked quickly with a younger
brother through byways, hurrying
to a neighbor's root cellar
or upstairs annex. You and I were ten
the year they crossed the border.
I've seen the story in glossy black and white:
old women at the ice cart buying fish
wrapped in a tattered paper. Once
while delivering bread for grandmother

3

you heard a piano. You stayed
beneath the rich man's windows,
made yourself late to dinner:
faces around the big table
joyous, though rumors
sizzled like meat beneath their songs.

At the same moment that I
sat at my school desk, you were grasped
by the collar. Flung to earth, a soldier
in a greatcoat. Bruises
on your thighs. While I repeated

je suis, tu es. I am. You were.
In the schoolyard
I cried: the boy who hated me

spat in my face, cursed
my mothers and fathers.
In that instant you

could have been taken out of time.
Or not: you might have fought.
Or escaped during the thirty days.
Changed sides, married one of them.
Maybe you always wear long sleeves
to hide a number. I think

you keep moving as I do,
throw the shuttle of your eyes
back and forth over faces, certain
that someday you will look
and recognize yourself. At night

or in a pondering of light.
When jagged parts seal over. When
it becomes hard to keep the beat.
By now we've traveled far, rag after rag
thrown down with toothbrushes,
with shoes and tins of shoe polish
still there, in mythic quantities. Small
heroic objects. And when I see them
when I see the pictures
from the camps

I don't marvel that I live, but ask
which one is me?

WINTER IN FOX-LIGHT

Under the flat sky a fox drags herself
to the edge of a brushwood.
New snow etches the shape
of each brown leaf, each
naked spray of twigs. He sees she is
shot in the spine: flailing, half-

paralyzed, white rings around the stones
of her eyes. A red cloak lays itself down for her
on the snow. Each flake stands out an instant
before it touches the dye.

Beneath the skin of her belly
a delicate jostling, as she
loses life. Quickly he slivers his knife point in

below the ribs, peels the thin wall back
like a grapefruit rind. He slits the muscled sack,

releases two cubs head-to-tail,
their blunt, tender clay. With his scarf
he dries the lacquered fur, zips them warm and squeaking
inside his jacket. They squirm against his chest
the three miles to the house, through a sky
that is reassembling itself on the land, everything
enveloped in the rush to bury

stubble, bury remnants; to bury all the broken
seedlings, their shapes rounding into identical drifts;
all the nests of summer hurled to the ground.

6

ECLIPSE

Leaves flicker, and suddenly the field
gathers into a knot—a deer

raises its head out of blackberry bushes,
its wide ears spoons for tasting danger. Still
as the deer, I return
its rapt gaze.

The red garage vanishes,
the cropped straw between us, the pine.

How long we balance
on the verge of becoming
neither one thing nor the other.

We wait, dusk
pressing away day moment by moment.

I hold my breath before the narrowing
of a margin, not because I
of the two of us
                am safe

but because I too could plummet.

SEEING DOUBLE

for my mother

Bearded with icicles: the black core
of a hill blown out to make a road straight.
Each mile I haven't seen for years,
every field vanished under last night's
early snowfall, long ago beat its image
into my mind for safekeeping.

Present and past jam each other, I can see
the static. I focus and refocus,
as on a line drawing of a staircase—
a sudden look snaps it inside out, shakes
my balance like a dog with a rabbit.
So this quiet landscape buckles inward

with a hollow thump, projected by memory
onto the screen inside my head, where I am
a child carried in a car through this same
countryside, past the Durland house,
the Murowski's barn, past fences like
map lines drawn over the land's white paper.

The view may be picturesque, for all I know.
I pinpoint each site in a too-familiar album
(my aunt and I in the back seat unwrapping
the china tea set she brought me from the City
here, right here, as we passed, *as I pass*
the icehouse pond I skated on)

and the next moment—or the same moment—
the pond is distant and gelid, a perfect postcard.
Who knows what the winter paintings of
Breughel, of Sisley conceal, what horror
of coziness, what fixation on pattern. Branches
sketch themselves in charcoal against a white

hillside; in the foreground, penciled
hatchings of star thistle. I could see this
as a *scene*. These rinsed-together memories
are prototypes of looking, their simulacra
densely packed into my life.
I drive past our old house. Behind it

a deer wearing his brown coat hangs
upside down by one hind leg from a tree.
The other legs and head stick stiffly
out from the body, as if spastic—no,
as if frozen: the deer is being punished.
The house has reverted to type; I park

on the curbless street, step back over
dark translucent shapes of bootsoles to school.
The door with its brass pull has a weight
my arm remembers. Up the concrete stairs, I find
the first-grade room, the second-grade room.
There are new desks but the same

clock. Out in the schoolyard I tread unspoiled
snow over the footprints I made when small.
The atoms of my childhood were fissionable
material; double vision can't bring back
their half-life. No stereoscope's knob
will sharpen this focus, merge these frames.

9

JOKE

Today in a parking lot
between a laundromat and pizza parlor
I heard *The Magic Flute* coming
from a car radio—the door wide open
and a man in a plaid shirt
sprawled, mending something under the dashboard.
It made me happy,

the way passing under a certain sycamore
bleached cream and citrine in patterns
where the old bark sloughed off
makes me happy—its torso
vaulting upward
into an empyrean of leaves—

Only the thin film of cirrus beyond

keeps me from levitating.
Did God mean anything by it,
giving us a soul—or was it

an accident, a joke—to break us out of
the hyphen between our birth and death dates?
Some comedian whisks us into

the sky, knowing the sky will not save us
but swing us airy as balloonists,
the colored silk belling us awake.

THE DISTANCE TO THE OCEAN

1

It is summer. She holds
her brother's hand, they walk slowly
the length of the driveway, edged with lemon balm.
They have been sent out with a game of jacks
to the concrete near the fishpond. *I have
a companion, I who have been
a cloud, a stone, a drop of water.*

A child tries to memorize
the ball she clutches,
the gravel driveway, yellow with sun,
the words *balm, morning, brother.*
She hems the words in, not to let them
sink into the water or ignite
in air. She must keep them

from now on, while jacks are being scattered
by a dog chasing a squirrel, and while rain
begins to fall on the concrete
in dark pennies, and onto the fishpond
with a sound of plucked strings.

2

Huge brown and white cows
bump softly against each other's flanks,
their pink bags shrunk with early milking.
In the wood beyond the brook the neighbor children
stifle laughter. They will never,
till all of them are grown, tell her
what they've been up to—though she
will ask again and again. Too
scared of the slippery plank
to cross with the others, she stays
with cow-haunches and cow-smell
till one of the beasts lifts its horns and bellows
and she sees for the first time
her own empty shape, arms outstretched, tottering
on a narrow beam.

3

Beyond dry fields, a gate
cut into a hedge. She pushes
against the gate. Bleeding hearts glimmer
among fringed leaves. At the edge of a pond,
under willows, women wash their hair. Sounds fall
from their mouths into the water.

Is that all I missed? But the garden
is full of artifice—stone deer, shrubs
in the form of urns. This may be only
a version of loss. Here in this garden
she puts hands on the nettle, feels
the unfolding of columbine
in the burrs of late August.

4

We move from the interior over straw
and animal droppings, the low sun
binding us in its amethyst bands. She suspects
that none of this is innocent.
                        But you,
my partner, my ally, who are you
to whom at certain moments I turn as though
to retrieve what I so eagerly
gave up, as though you
hold it safe. She has reached
the ocean. She lets the tide carry her out.

What shakes beneath her feet
as she pulls herself back through the surf
is neither earth nor water.
In the night sky
a knot loosens;
birds drop out of the moon.
One by one
trees are felled
and stars attached to the roots
descend in fading arcs.
The trees must know
what is happening.

On the cliff over the sea,
a black cypress: to name it
is to charge it with irony. A wave
hurtles over itself, glittering, lethal.
Beneath everything, the black, pelagic water
that never sees light.

899 MONTGOMERY STREET

Every night I buried my head in the pillow
at my cousin Norman's, not to hear
his cries through the wall, or my aunt's voice
catching and splintering on them.
Next morning the kitchen,

its cool white tiles to the ceiling,
the fire escape at the window.
I learned stickball
and in return Norman would

play Hansel to my Gretel.
We drew the blinds, then hand in hand
followed a trail we couldn't see. My younger
brother was the witch; I thrust
on this new brother, Hansel, wishes
that rasped at the edge of my hunger.
Forcing ourselves through fine

and then finer sieves, we came out
washed clean, tranquilized. Then
we pulled the cords of the blinds,
grew slowly coarse again
in daylight. I never asked

about his enormity, his punishment.
Every night my cousin's cries
dug into my chest like a spade.
I can still feel them turn over in me,
jagged and unclean, summoning harm
from all its points of entry.

MESSENGER

We take it slow and easy
as though the road, winding shady
with eucalyptus and willow,
will be gone tomorrow and we'll have to rely
on memory. Leaves
push up through the paving,
knock-kneed fences slant alongside. Reflex

stops us: suspension
of heartbeat, of drawn breath,
as if the world, like us struck
immobile, is disengaged from time
by an apparition,

a peacock
shimmering his blue neck, shaking
all his jewels at us.
The small elegant head twitches, and we

are without words
as he bends slowly under a fence
and vanishes,
drawing divinity after him like a tail.

HOW MUSIC PREPARES US FOR THE WORLD

for Susanna

A stone winery: backdrop. Musicians
on the terrace. Ranges of hills.
A spacious lawn with harebells and cyclamen,
wicker hampers, blankets. Off stage water
trickles over rocks, I can hear it
in the pauses. People wait
for something to happen.

My daughter is seated on the terrace. She wears
the same skirt, orchestra-black, I made her at fifteen.

Summer-jacketed men, women
in muted colors wander back and forth
greeting friends. One woman sits reading on
the grass, I would like her to be reading
Chekhov. Others stand
near a table arrayed with wineglasses
or walk incautious over the lawn scattering
drops, a full glass in each hand.

My daughter talks to a player behind her. (The long gesture
of her raised arm, curving into
the body's half-spiral.) Flash of sun
on a bottle, on a knife—someone cutting,
cutting bread from a picnic basket—

17

and the present moment stabs open,
as though all I see were painted on a transparent scrim.

The music, soon to start, is soon over,
which is why I love the sound of water; everything
happening at once.

It is August, it is twilight.
I want to avert my eyes: a man at the curb
hunched into the dark heap of his body.

I want her to move away from
this street, not carry her violin
through these narrow nights. I'm no saint,
it could make me callous; her too.
I take in the claustrophobic moment.

Once I held a basin for a drunk
but he was in my house and his arms didn't work.
I caught his winy vomit, steeling myself.
Knew there was no merit to it
because I didn't do it with love, only
distaste, only pity. Street a dirty string

through the middle of a block. Silvered iron gates
shutting off concrete stairways.
A citron streetlight. I wish

she would move away from here.
I sit in the locked car waiting for her.
Out of the corner of my eye I see
young men in twos and threes hanging out
in front of the buildings.
But I don't look. Around here, she says,
looking is like wearing a diamond,
you could be stabbed for it. We do not
hear music now, but only half a mile away

a tenor singing Schubert, in
eyeglasses and a swallowtail coat,
will reveal himself the genius
of water, father of wishes—
when love is released from sorrow—each tone
the essential footstep
on a flat stone crossing a streambed.

Later she and I will sit
with drinks at a sidewalk cafe. Everyone
out of doors to draw breath will take
breath away with them from the warm summer night.
Beyond an iron rail
a derelict, he's black, shambles by,
in a cracked baritone singing away
the privacy he was born with. He stops
before a black man in tennis whites
at the next table. The tune
flattens out, the words go on: *Dirt is*

dirt, junk is junk, I come in wrapped in a
sack and go out whole and new. He leans over
the rail, not touching it. Expressionless,
the seated man puts two fingers into
his wallet, hands over a folded bill.

She whispers to me later she knows how he felt, she hates
the way he must have churned inside.

〰️

Harebells, cyclamen. Hills beyond
with cypress and oak.
We don't have to say why we are moved.
The concertmaster turns to the strings
and bows a long A. The conductor
taps the stand.

                         She may or may not know
she is playing for me. (Once I, center aisle,
was surely the only one in the world
who could see her strong slender fingers
in the organist's mirror, flashing
like rapids: I would know those bright birds
anywhere. Flowers dehiscing. Schools of flying fish.)

And we fill this chamber, reaching
for fulfillment, for simultaneity—

How can we earn the melody's bright thread
that ties us to each other, shelters us
in the lee of such fragility.

IT LOOKS LIKE UP

But it frightens me, the duck family
paddling into oblivion,
the bright blistering waves, sun
glaring them out of the universe.

Baby birds hatch without eyes, their beaks
cross like scissors.

I thought *the worse things get*
the quicker they're bound to reach a turning point
so leave it alone.

There is a kind of tree called
pernambuco, it grows
only in the Amazon and is cut into
violin bows. It bends, it sings. Investors
lock it in their vaults, driving up the song.

Things can get worse and we
slide after.
I stop myself
from going out any more
to the bad news, from saying
let it hit me, we'll go to the bottom
and then begin to rise.

There is this one swath of water...you
look: it blinds you as hell blinds you.
You are falling off the edge of it,
you are being swallowed.

23

II

It is the best joke there is, that we are here, and fools—that we are sown into time like so much corn, that we are souls sprinkled at random like salt into time and dissolved...The joke part is that we forget it.

—Annie Dillard, Holy the Firm

THE LADDER

Charles was reaching down to pick up
something from the ground, I believe
it was a spoon. He swayed
on the rickety wooden
ladder, the one we used to use
to lean into the pear trees.
He should have used the new
aluminum ladder, shouldn't
have leaned down to pick up
the spoon, or been caulking
the lintels in his suit. And when I
looked through the window and saw him
reaching, amusing the others below,
I had only time to think
it's all up now, the signs
have been bad and this
is why, for in that moment the ladder
wheeled smoothly, with a slow
grandeur, and Charles, already
leaning over, hadn't far
to go, but it was far enough
to open our whole world
and throw us down with him
into a broken place, raw and tangled,
only a step from where we thought we lived.

A WAY OUT OF THE PICTURE

Raphael's "Saint Margaret," Vienna

1

Light-burnished in a depth of darkness,
craggy rocks, misshapen trees—

                                   a woman
caught in a huge serpent's windings
that shine like beaten metal.
I stare. I too

stand within a monster's coil. Death
has come near enough

to let me smell its breath. That voracious craw
craning back on itself. The coral gorge
tunnels to black, roars for her flesh
under its melting blue silk tunic; Raphael's brush

sculptures the nipple of one breast as she
turns; the other is in darkness.

But this is myself
on the museum wall: the surgical scar
still tightens when I lift my arm.
She astounds me—this serene woman,
her inward glance—

I snatch at symbols where I find them.

28

Knee bending into the bulging belly,
she gazes without fear
at the maw that gapes itself inside out.
The hilted object in her left hand—not
a knife or dagger, but to the young woman,
weapon enough.
I am the one who must invent
strength to gaze steadily
at jaws ready to snap, must invent a valor
weightless as the cloak she carries, its red flare
fitting the shape of joy at her center.

2

          How to imagine her
reaching this plane...I call up a sky,

not Raphael's blue, but one sullen
with clouds. She has forced herself between
granite slabs, past giant roots cramping
from fissures, into a rock-swept
landscape. Let's say she slips,
nearly loses her foothold,

          but catches herself,
grapples a rock by the shoulder.
Twisting round she sees a cave
where candles flicker into a vanishing depth,
then blink out one by one. Candle smoke
rasps her throat until the last flames
die away; not only the cave but the whole zone
goes dark—the rock, the path.

The world no longer resists her.

3

When we see her in the painting, her vision
has turned. Her passage among the rocks
is behind her; she doesn't look
the roaring monster in the throat

for nothing, into those black depths splaying
to pink. By the time Saint Margaret
encounters the serpent, death
is her salt, her bread. But what of
me, will I know how to do

what none of us has done?
When the beast's nostrils
sniff horribly at my leg, will they sniff
cowardice? Or will I find a way
to the joy that shimmers at the center:
red for determination; blue
for the immaculate garment
repeated in the trapezoid of sky

                               that opens
a way out of the picture, the consummation of the
struggle being the only way out of the struggle
we do not discover until we have passed through it.

THIS TIME, THIS PLACE

Monet's Series Paintings, Art Institute of Chicago

You walk through oat fields and poppies
and oat fields at twilight,
grain stacks, melting snow
and grain stacks just before sunset
and seven poplars seen at midday and the same
seven, banks of the Epte, twilight,
the curve of the spirit
that had gone unnoticed as you
walked, that carried you
in a swirl of branches—each time
a slight difference of angle, of daylight
through these poplars
over this river, the Epte,
one view slightly more hazy,
and some believe
each view is meant to capture
an earlier or later moment
in the probably futile but staggering
attempt to render all the moments—
try this, try me out, see

if I can deliver up my moments—see if you
can see what skulks behind;
if these slim trunks are not really cracks
in the lavender horizon,
cracks that let darkness show
through the lavender air

ANNIVERSARY: *the Capay Valley in February*

The year I thought I would die
almond blossoms granted me a plenitude

that held all my longing
in the cupped palm of one moment.

I felt kin to the bees, their dive
into color and scent, flurry

that deflowers the senses—a richness
I had to teach myself to leave,

to transmute—through some
reverse alchemy that hummed around me—

into an unremarkable metal
I could bear to part from,

as though letting go of something
could impart its own solace.

An eternal greenness
antlers out from my forehead

each spring—always taken by surprise—
I stroll these orchards, flush

with new grass, mustard, chickweed
cresting the furrows. Almond petals,

33

white and urgent, sugar the ground
before I realize another February is

upon us. These buzzing blooms
unsettle my weather, unchink

the seals I've daubed over memory
that let me pretend

the now is normal; the here
common as sparrows. The ferment

that years ago freed joy
from the hold death had on me

baffles me still when I ask
how to live up to it.

LAPSED AGNOSTIC

I want no bargains with life, I demand
no miracles, and therefore
will not file my soul for safekeeping
among banks of lilies, among choirs of seraphim
that promise the leaves off the jacaranda trees.

        Yet how I love
singing processions, moments
of transfiguration on the faces of the religious
as they kiss their prayerbooks,

                love the madonnas of Botticelli
with their assailable lips, azure mantles
falling in broken scallops from room to room
as they offer the lofty, moon-round breast,
an imaginable white drop blooming at the nipple—

        How I love all
who lay their gifts on altars, love
all parting with oneself for love—

following, or not, a gossamer cord
into the infinite. Contracts with gods
are not that different from those
with the devil: pay

at the beginning or pay in the end. Caught
between straight lines of the old duality—
they may be ornate, handcarved, rubbed
with gold leaf; they may frame the face
incomparably, but anyone can toss rings at you

35

and win a plush duck. Imagine
stringing all the birds of the mind
on a thread of belief—

Yet I too yearn

for Piero's frescoed air, his saints'
smooth limbs—the way I yearn,

standing in a field of rustling grasses,
for that sight, that sound, to fill me,
lusting after beauty as though I were a god.

WAITING FOR THE CRANES

Whether it was the four geese and a swan floating
on the wet glass of sloughs and canals
that ease the Sacramento
toward the sea—

or whether, on a rise overlooking
the delta's sinuous geography, it was the young man
sitting on a pickup's flatbed, one arm
draped around a Lab's shoulders
and a pair of field glasses
in the other hand;

or whether
it was simply the waiting—

for we had come early, past
the stench of neglected cattle
standing in slime to their fetlocks—
had come past, or rather through,
the delta itself, whose protoplasmic light
picks up and is changed by all it looks on,
the young man showing us
belted kingfisher, white-tailed kite, phoebe;
saying he comes for the quiet, as this place

hasn't been ruined yet,
the three of us scouring the sky
for the sandhill cranes' late afternoon landfall—
this marsh where they spend each night,
tule clumps lipping patches of water—
and so I thought it must have been the waiting

that readied us for a sign, he
explaining in his rancher drawl
how black bill and trombone voice
distinguish tundra swans from their whistling
cousins, and graceful plumage
sets a great blue heron apart from

the bulky bald-pate birds
we were watching for,
until a primordial call

at last belted down from far-off throats—
more and more of the cranes
working in heavily
from a band on the eastern horizon,
blotching and peppering a sunset
that now flamed the whole sky-
reflecting delta as though to hold us
in its ruby palm—

and then I knew it was
the rapt look on the young man's face
that let this lift
from our baffled longing: a sense
that something might be healed—

as the coiled lengths of the cranes'
windpipes that spiral like French horns under the breastbone
filled the sky
with a blast from the Eocene.

FRAGILE

A tightly sealed package.
Inside, a glass goblet
packed in solid white
bubbles. You could
throw it from the roof and it
would bounce. Imagine
the crystal within the box, and then
within the crystal, like
unspun filaments inside
a spider, a structure. Lines
on which things break.
Lines that come from nowhere, fracture lines
along which the crystal, one day
gently lowered into lukewarm water
will sing and come apart.
Like icebergs, like
lightning. Each thing
will have its breaking day.

MADAME MONET IN THE GARDEN

The artist's wife
        sits in an oval of light
                beneath a pear tree,

her dress spread out about her
        on the grass.
                Sun falls

like petals through the tree.
        In fact you don't know
                whether the pale dots that dapple her

are petals or sunshine;
        it's conceivable
                she sits sprinkled with pear blossoms

she doesn't brush away.
        You watch,
                waiting to see what will happen.

She gazes beyond
        the boundary you can see, perhaps
                beyond the garden.

You turn away
        to look at another painting,
                thinking to give her

scope to raise her arm,
        flutter it—see
                whether something may fall.

By the time you whirl back,
       her hand is once more
              motionless in her lap,

brushed with more petals,
      or scraps
            of the same sunlight.

THE ROAD TO GIVERNY

Each petal
is distinct, the cool air does not vibrate;
if I am about to walk
into a painting, it is not

Monet's. His fierce dismantling of vision…
inviting me into a world that exists

but not among these lindens, these
iris, any place the hand can touch.

I stop three women walking together
to ask if the path does in fact
lead to Giverny, and they tell me
not to let my *sac* hang loosely from my shoulder,
but to clutch it in both arms.

We are given more than resides
in the trees and shrubs, in the iris
leaning, stretching into the path,
and, riding the water beneath
the Japanese bridge, the flowers
the French call nymphs.

This happened later, at the station.
A breakneck jamming against me from the rear,
slam of a stocky body like a pistol. Then
he was gone, my wallet with him.

42

Not much in it, but I can still feel
how his body pitched me hard
against the turnstile. Anything

can come down out of the flies at random.
It may not mean a thing.
I put my hand in my pocket
and find

a hand there. Or sipping a drink
wonder what's wrong—
Scum on the water, dirt in the
beer...? I look at the glass,
and it's the rim broken off
in one clean sharp

ring, I'm leaking
blood, tongue and lip, broken
glass in the mouth. Simple

disasters: I catch myself thinking, falsely:
the tax one pays, a tithe. A sign.

As I looked back
I saw him, angry-looking, short, beefy.
What can keep us from harm—
you, me, him.

From the bridge multitudes of flowers
like cupped hands
curve upward.

This is as far as we've come.

LIGHTHOUSE AT POINT REYES

Fog settles in
like blindness,
muffles every sound
but the pronged blast
that splinters the air
like a hurled pitchfork.
I lean against
an iron rail, watching
gulls and cormorants
fade in and out.
At the cliff's base
long sleeves of surf
erode each other
as they break on shore.
Fungus and algae
paint the rocks
rust, khaki, yolk.
Jellyfish ghost
the water's surface.
The old-time keepers
trimmed wicks, filled lamps.
They tugged lanterns
up the steep risers
of a narrow spiral,
polished lenses
that scalloped
the shining cupola
like giant fish scales.
Storms battered loneliness
against the inside
of their skulls,

44

the foghorn and its echo
their only companion.
Something out there
on which the sound resounds
—something more than water—
throws back the double note.
Not the flat invisible
horizon, not the lowering
sky, so close
you could almost
touch it if you tried.

THE TURNING

A horse blows into bright grass,
spiders are born, the sun
lifts stones from the river.
Tomorrow's moon
leaps off the white edge.

On the river bank an old pair stroll.
A child dawdles after them, his hands
like an old woman's: small parched trees.
Years of labor might have splayed them like that.

A thug puts down the lumbering shape of his body,
the brown of the river is troubled.
And then he comes partly out of the water:
he shakes himself and leaves the water.
He looks in their direction.
Something one turns away from
comes over his face.

If he should raise his hand against them...

There is no sky, there can be no end,
only the mother and father falling softly, only
the child turning, arms and legs in a giant pinwheel.

46

HUNGER STRIKE

for Bobby Sands

The early days were bad.
Wild pigs came to his cell, they tore
at his belly's indifference. Slight of build,
he could still
seize a pig by the teeth
when it opened its jaw. He would knuckle and
knee it to the floor till it knew enough
to stop struggling.

At that time
he spoke to no one, not even
his brother. For days he stayed down
with one knee in a boar's thick throat
till it grew mild,
licked his hand
and ambled out of the cell,
dust still on its back.
Later he wore a bandage over his eyes.

What do we know. Hunger
is wanting dinner. But the eyes
wobbling crazily in the seventh week,

bones that pierce the flesh,
the burning away of all
except consciousness … The wild pigs
came back, slunk out again.
He foresaw new graves
dissolving to mud in rain, lines
of innocents. But he was forging a logic.
Each day more of him belonged to the light
and less to his keepers: what was not consumed
still burns.

THE COUNTRY OF HOPE

This is a strange
country. A ship full of people
drifts offshore, not allowed to land.
On the boardwalk the knife-thrower's wife,
veiled below arabesque eyes, is tied to a wall.
There's a mermaid, never out of water before.
Her tail flops in the dirt.

What we want:
to choose our element. We're tied,
we are dragged over rock and sand.
All we think of: how to break away.
We have only one chance.

The ship
hovers near shore, never mooring.
The knife-thrower holds still, aims.
The woman's outline bristles with steel.
She's been sullen with him. He's thinking
of drawing blood.

I see how we carry
hope around without knowing it.
Melody and harmony hold us in their hands.
They curl after each other, not
sounding together. He throws the knife
straight for the center. That is only
our signal. We are ready
to leap into our life with one burst,
we are listening for improbable music.

AT THE END OF THE CENTURY

after Jules Goncourt

Yes, savagery. We need it, every four
or five hundred years. Or the world
will die of civilization.
So I will not betray

the time I am born into, no, not the stolen
rose, deep original red like the disappearance
of history. You look and you look: how
could the rose be gone, its stout canes.
Thorns that would pierce leather.
In fog, in cold, in wind it bloomed,
that blackred velvet. Yet
the hole gouged in the ground

is not peculiar to our time: time out of mind
we've come along with spades and barrows
and dug. The need was that great.

Nor will I betray infants left in alleyways—
there have always been unwanted
young, their faces turned down
into the ashes, a choking in the throat.
Such children if they live will refuse
nothing. They weigh with us so slightly
in the balance. I will not
turn my back on them, or on seabirds
washing up on beaches. Soon

we will be purged; we will be primed
for the deep red tinge a fine Burgundy
leaves on the palate, we will be
clean and ready to keep faith
with burial and leakage on the lesser avenues.
Yes, I will stand loyally by
the paradigms of our time, the slow death

of machines, the clean-shaven Amazon banks
where jaguars lie, swelling and whitening
in the shadeless light.

GRACE

This is what I once expected:
if you tried, you could get
something for something. The ice cream cone
after the dentist. A gold star for no mistakes.
Now I ask only

to see a certain late afternoon blue
knife into the ocean.

At the window, sunset. The lights
are on; I part the curtains.

What I want is knowledge.

        In the midst of
tearing, being torn from—
our work goes on. Wrecking
the city, building over rubble,
till we are left

with the ordinary shape of things. The wind
filling their clothes on the line,
white and pleadings of white, as though
they could return.

Heavy dusk under the trees.
I open the door.
The sky has hoarded brightness
like armfuls of lilac.

I walk to the cliff. Color still touches
the edge of the sea; shadows show

where the light is coming from.
How hard it is, the work we have to do

to earn the body of light that carries us
toward whatever stays visible after dark.

III

Till the bridge you will need be form'd, till the ductile anchor
hold,
Till the gossamer thread you fling catch somewhere ...

—*Walt Whitman, "A Noiseless Patient Spider"*

IMPROVISATION

You sit in a theater, focusing
on light. All around
it is dark, you are dark. You watch
a world give birth to itself
on a white dinner plate, an uncovered
bed, a sunlit terrace. This
is what it says: all of you
sitting there are shadows.

How would it feel not to be
borrowed—a shadow—grey paper
creasing over the edges of stairs.
This impulse to plunge into the open,
thrust your bones into your own
shape, cram every curve

full. Light and dark will
touch each other. You have no idea
what you will meet face to face, who
will appear as though from the pit
to announce:

> *the beginning*
> *I was only waiting for this*
> *the lights, the lights!*

AMONG TREETOPS

To realize you can do it
is the hard thing about flying—

One minute you're stuck to the floor;
the next

your toes begin to arch and flex
in irresistible leaps.
You practice—

and discover a sudden knack of lofting into midair.

It takes trust: that your bones
will lift your flesh. At that point
to fly becomes not only possible

but inescapable—and I'm not talking

about some cloth or aluminum contrivance
from which you dangle,
in hope. I'm not talking

about a jump from heights.
This is about generating more feeling
than you can account for,

58

like the fizz of spring.
If you possess it, you've no choice
but to glide about the room
six feet off the ground. You look
for a window, maneuver the up-
drafts, gently bump
the chandelier—until
you find yourself

                  among treetops.
Your flights lengthen
and become a way to live.
Face to face with entropy,
you are still rising.

FULL DAY

Morning sun and coffee and rolls on the deck
and the umbrella training its long shadow
over the rail as we toasted the day
in three colors—
plum tree, alder, cypress.
Up on the wire a hummingbird settled,
still as an owl.

            The day before
I'd pushed barrowfuls of rank
leafage and clods the roots wouldn't relinquish,
and the clear view I made
of myrica and wild radish
seemed worth a full day:

and so when sin
crawled out of the roof gutter
and dropped on my shoulders in today's mild gold,
I felt I'd been opened
and something heavy and gritty
poured into me, something
I couldn't get rid of,
that made my body slump
like a thing I was hauling
through wet sand.

I saw illumined
in the dark that fell around me
not only the ruined morning, but—

as though my life had just begun and
I'd stepped down from
heaven directly into hell—
the question of my own worth:
the harsh choice of swallow or choke.

And felt a kind of summons
at the steep pitch of my
descent—the way it fit
into a cosmic ecology: the road up
was long, I could not see the end,
the work lay ahead.

A VIEW OF THE LAGOON

It helps to think
how cloud shadows look, the sand spit
a rim for the lagoon's shallow basin,
surf that stamps its hoof
on the hard shore. It helps the way

I've been feeling this summer.
Words fling me all ways at once:
blessed are the dumb
who don't learn from their own history,
like skidding into the guard rails
on an oil slick in sudden rain.
You try to force the steering

against the car's will; your hands
in spasm on the wheel
transmit no traction to the road.

Entanglement is not like a gardenia;
you give the man
a dollar, dip the petals
into cool water. You know
where you stand, it smells heavenly
for a day and a half. It helps

to remember the look
on the face of a beggar
to whom a passerby
drinking espresso in styrofoam
extended Chinese takeout. Joy
showered the street like money.

To remember the lagoon's stillness
under a clotted sky. Somewhere

tiered hills recede behind fog veils.
Somewhere an empty rowboat lies unmoored,
beached in marsh grass, with a look
of being about to be come back to.

PERIOD OF GRACE

Sun nets combers, rocks, fishing boats
in its dazzle—their etched masts and lines—
and pelicans flapping brown and angular,
ready to snap shut in a dive
terse as a knife.

       Between hell and absolution, I walked down
       Terrace Road, saw fog lick the distance
       clean of sea. Oak and laurel
       patterned tawny hills behind the bay
       through openings scissored by cypress.

The keen smell of the sea, of fish:
too much for me to swallow.
In this summer of making war and
peace with myself, all I want
is to receive the wide stretch,
the ample shine. I walk barefoot
where torn spills of foam
slap themselves down on the sand.

       Sun kindled a bank of nasturtium
       that burned unconsumed.

On top of one of the little sand waves
that the wind makes, a white chiton shell
scoured of turquoise by salt and sun
balances like a butterfly,
its blotches shaping a death's-head.

ATTENTION

A hundred meters above the Pacific—
that aquamarine, that jazz blue sky,
chevrons and trapezoids skating
toward a scumbled streak
of fog on the horizon—

we talked of I don't know what,
walked without noticing

past a slope where a rivering wind
braids heavy grasses into undulations
the colors of sacking, of parrots, lizards, lions.
A grove of tall eucalyptus beyond,
and falling away from those
the sea.

My pen lines white paper with ink,
the window screen's graph
strains tangles of brush outside.
Second sight gives me

the field's ventilating light,
blown silk the slow hawks make
of sky, its gloss below
that wipes white arcs
onto the beach. Yet
even when I think I'm
present, an inadvertence

like the blur where sea becomes sky
takes me and washes me
in its ringing vessel, walks me
away from there unchanged.

PACT

But the angels don't need souls
because they never needed to choose; we
who do not live in a realm of unmediated light
constantly strive to reach the light, as, say,
at a country inn with friends, when
having driven through forested terrain
to a clearing with rough benches and tables,

we gather ourselves tightly inside our clothes
too thin for the day's sudden chill, all of us
laughing, rubbing our elbows.
A waitress who speaks a foreign language
brings out a tray of beer and bread and meats
in the cool overcast afternoon,
and all we want is to breathe deeply
of the forest air, to see
between the slender trees vineyards laid
over the lap and knees of the landscape.
Leafy branches close to our faces
cut the sky into shapes. A shape
like a hand illuminated from the back
offers, holds something out—

Say that on a certain day
you're running as though you've grown
inches taller in the night, the air
streaming under your bare soles.
A skater among walkers,
you're almost at a goal
that seemed unreachable,

and then within an ace of arriving
you realize it's not what you want at all:
what if you stop; what if you turn back?

We let ourselves believe we
are the ones it was given to choose—
everything we were to become,
without corruption and without fruit.
Though in fact there was no promise,
the future did not exist

until we put it into our heads.
We hunger to transform what's been lost,
we go about gathering up
the scattered bits,
having stripped ourselves

of the calm protection granted the other
animals, the forest icons in their white pelts,
white deer spotted with gold. You can see them
only at dusk, in the woods below the second meadow,
the path's canopy darkening around your head.
You can't quite believe
the hushed light you glimpse through the trees
can be white deer browsing. What are they,
these mild animals disguising themselves
as angels? We did not ask Prometheus
to bring us fire, did not know
how it would hurt. Oh those names,

that flight from harmony—
that cutting loose—

68

LOVING A MATHEMATICIAN

The ether, or whatever's up there—
some infinite glassy staircase—
crackles for you
with truth, with beauty—and I
have never followed you even to
the second rung. I used to think Pi
was just a way of measuring circles.
You tell me now that Pi dwells
in gaseous, in liquid universes
where there are no circles, where rings
couldn't form if I dropped a pebble.
For there are no pebbles either—
no discs no balls no equators,
only pure structure.
It's true, you say,
that Pi always turns up,
like an old irrational uncle
who's been traveling round the country
doing card tricks. But circles
are only one of his arts:
Pi rolls his thumb through the ink
of odd numbers; from his hiding place in
square roots under square roots like
a wagonload of deviant potatoes
Pi shines traces beyond
the galaxies mathematicians map,
haunts the void between electrons,
stalks black holes and red shifts.
Inching like a growing crystal
into cosmic chinks, Pi waits
for thought to close in, waits

69

to be pounced on with a pencil
as his secrets repercuss
into patient, searching minds.
I ask you this: does Pi buckle
the whole universe together?
Can Pi be God?

For the first time I believe
I could follow you up and up—

THE ORDINARY

Silk heaviness of the bed—
we make ourselves languid
with sun and sea and our opalescent

mingling, our breath . . . and what is it
we are still trying to finish?
Stay sane by imagining

this picture: he makes cinnamon toast
while she reads a story to the child.
It's bedtime, she sits on the side

of the bed. The child kneels slightly behind her
to look at the pictures. One arm
crooks over her shoulder;

the hand resting against her cheek
as though to soothe her
soothes her.

If dailiness ebbed away I'd burn
bright white, a lump of phosphorus
lifted from its water bath.

Now the first nights of winter,
first moments of dusk.
When it was youth that pleasured me

I had not the least idea
what love is,
it was myself

I loved. And us
as budding fruit trees, apricot,
coming into blossom.

Love filled me
with the idea of love
as *something that could*

happen to me, that could unscroll
from a seashell, enter like the dove
of the Annunciation, its spotless wings

shivering with bliss.
Instead the ordinary
stretches and atomizes love

until it envelops
everything we happen to; opens us
toward the indwelling, salt stars.

WHITE CLAY CREEK, APRIL

At a bend where the creek widens and
        stills, Tom shows Justin
                how to skip stones,
and we count their diminishing

stutters. Deer foraging
        in a distant meadow
                lift their heads in our
direction, turn mineral.

Five-year-old Rhoda flings
        a handful of sand into the creek.
                As it clouds to the bottom
she makes a wish,

the way we did last Rosh Hashanah
        when we emptied our pockets
                to let the current
do its cleansing work. Now, with Rhoda,

we make wishes again.
        Justin, who's eight, looks hard
                at what he's found
in the path's scrabbled sand—possibly

an arrowhead: *I'm shaking; I'm so excited*
        I could never
                be an archeologist,
I'd be shaking all the time.

A great horned owl
        whirs into sky the muted lavender
                of those summer evenings
when parents called from an incandescent room

come in, come inside. Justin wants us
        to turn back,
                as though he were alone
in the gathering dark—

and I ponder
        a child's certainty
                that nothing
can protect you.

My wish: not the impossible:
        not that we can hold
                this moment unmoving—
but, as we disburden ourselves

of what sifts of fallout
        we consign
                to the river,
that the moment may spin us out with its grace.

ANNIVERSARY

after Chagall

The loose-furled days of autumn
upon us. Cider tooth whistles from the
orchard, and in the unrolled wheatfield
the last of the slow sun
lets go its sweetness.
How do we live? We have used up
the old blasphemies—demand,
forgive—have come out
the other side. It is always, still,
the time just before we've learned
the rules, it's the time to soar,
time for trees and tall buildings
to weave themselves around
the wind, visible as a goddess, and we,
who've come this long migration
like wild geese, our necks
stretched out before us,
take our bearings by the stars.
We ask each other: ready?

ABOUT TIME

for Joshua

Smoke across the street spirals from
a chimney through almond blossoms,
rain pearls leafless twigs
outside my window. These
are the only hand space holds out
for me to grasp. I make myself dizzy
conceiving our swinging galaxy
as a single atom of some vast being
whose smallest fingernail I try
to imagine—while for some creatures
whose smallness won't stay down,
an atom of my own fingernail might be
their sun, moon and stars. I stagger,
then rise like a bubble: for if all
the suns and nebulae, and you and I,
spin like quarks and charms in some
nitrogen atom, then the sizzling sky that
stuns us on a clear night becomes a snug
living room by a fireside. I sprinkle
brown sugar on the bread and butter of
Arcturus' old light, squeeze lemon
on the old light of Betelgeuse, and think,
if space is this delicious, then what about
time? In one pencil dot we've come
out of the trees into cyberspace,
and while the abominable nail
scratches a mosquito bite we could
vanish. But what if our fleeting moment

is some thumbelina's long life; what if
her stellar everlasting barely nicks
our blip? If a ninety-degree tilt
can shift space into another dimension,
why not flip time on its side too,
jab it through the skin of what never
lasts, make it bleed, give it a torque
through the other side of consciousness
into what's neither a split nano-
second nor eternity itself: and this
will not be teatime. Straight ahead
death lurks, and our solace
is the angle of reflection we skew
off plumb, to impale for one moment
a moment: to seize what never stops—
a breath before it cracks the flame.

WALKING UP THE HILL

With a few quick strokes
a pine tree displays itself
in the right foreground.
Fishing boats like spiky water-insects
coast the sunlit bay,
their shiny gear dragging nets.
A pelican reconnoiters for fish
in a bare light the color of
sun skipping stones on the ocean.

From houses above the road, flights
of laughter and conversation
stir me, drops of white wine
shaken from a glass. I yearn
to be on a summer porch
that overlooks the sea, linking
loops of talk into meshes
with people I don't know.

The pelican's angular form
plummets heavily
into the waves. A woman
leads a Dalmatian down the hill,
her eyes on the horizon, where sea
and sky are rubbed to a half-tone
by a thumb of fog.
At the top of the hill
I have it, almost all.

Even among friends, I am often silent.

THE WATERFALL

Again and again
you used to dare the bridges,
looking straight ahead. One shaky log
led to another high above the rushing fork
from islet to mountainside. You climbed
out of aspen through pine, up bare boulders.
Higher, scarps of granite jutted; you began
to hear the water's insistent mutter.

First you tried
gentle slopes with footspace among clover.
Then reached impassable clefts. The tough
climb up the rock-torn steep took you out
upon the shoulder of the world. From cliff's
edge you looked across the chasm to a waterfall
flashing quicksilver as though thickets had parted
to let you see into their sealed center of light.

You imagined
being sprayed with its spindrift, stunned
by its thunder. But you would let yourself claim
only the remote sight of that ragged pouring light.

This time you follow
the pump station road to the creek's far side.
You climb up red rock, climb up granite; listen
for the whisper that becomes a roar. Zigzag
every inch of the mountainside and you will not
find it. There is only one way to the waterfall
and you have taken it.

PROGRESS REPORT

If you turn from this, there is nothing:

from apple trees, from a hand held out
before you. Once I thought that meant
nothing

was all there was,
and I was scared
out of my mind. They tried
to comfort me but you can't pluck belief
from the air or just find it
in your soup. I loved
the emerald-green tiny frog
that appeared at the garden tap each
morning; grey lichen frilling grey
rocks, that barked your fingernails
if you picked it off. I could sit
spellbound, watching a harpist
unreel her audible web. But

saw no reason these should matter.
Because we'd die. When one day
the sun swelled into a Red Giant
and then collapsed,

(a time we think about only
to glance tentatively at each other,
and smile by default)

(just as when I was a kid I said
in The Year Two Thousand I'll be …
—but I could never be as old as that!)

then if there were still our kind around,
offspring with race memory
of you—of me—a manner, say,
of hunching head into shoulders
when it thunders, or peaking up
the eyebrows in sympathy—all those things
we'd pass along to whoever was still there
when the sun shrank whitely—

then if we shrank along with it—
would it mean none of this mattered? Life

is what warms a room while not cooling itself;
we do what we do for more than survival,

if we're among the lucky ones.
For when asked by the secret police of his country
What will you do to help us? a friend, Sandor,
replied that Napoleon used donkeys in
his campaign. And invented sleeve buttons.
Taking Sandor for a simpleton they let him alone.
He carried his dead companion
eight miles on his back—the regiment's
law, but also the way of salvation:
first vision of a transformed universe.
As though vision is enough,
knowing how to go on is enough.
There is a young woman in this town

who walks as if a four-footed creature reared up
and miraculously discovered walking.
Seeing her from a distance you experience
slight shock; she gains ground slowly
and with determination. You and she

will pass each other; you nod and say hello
and she returns you a smile

that lavishes you with a cello's warmth,
urging to concord before it retreats
to dissonance again,

a vanishing personal song
that will flip darkness over
to its other side, the frail bridge

on which we travel toward each other.

ALL BUT THE BLACKBERRIES THEMSELVES

for Rebecca

There is the shiny beetleness of their
blackness and the sun implanting
roundness and blossoms belling forth
even more sweetness, and the wasps
insinuating. There are the first solitary
notes ringing the berry pail's thin metal
with a plangent clangor that soon becomes
soft drumming as we advance into the patch.
Its long arms barb us away, hook us close,
snag clothes, bramble flesh: draw blood,
mingle our scarlet with their crimson.
We leave on the vine all stubborn berries
that cling by one unripe drupelet, leave
the tight pinched greens, surly reds,
stone-seeded browns. Leave
the powdery overripe berries falling
or about to fall, and those half-eaten
by small mouth parts. For us there are only
the fat, the tender, the ink-black,
full-term, ready-to-pop berries
whose purples, flush with juice,
flaunt lavish and sun-warmed or hide
cool beneath dense leaves, heaping
the gorged container until at last
there is burden, there is nightmare—that
by reaching too far, trying too hard
we'll upend our gleaming plunder among

83

field stubble or its own thorned bed
and end up losing it all. And although
we already know that the more we have
the more we have to lose, there is
greed: greed of the nearly-filled pail,
for the last berry but one—but two—greed
for the berry not yet noticed—for whose sake
the arm with the pail stretches far behind
in balance—in arabesque—in pas de deux—
in succulence, in stain, in rapture—

A GAP IN THE DARK

They lined the girls up
one night at summer camp
and said to the loneliest of the boys
Choose one, Frenchie. He chose
Estelle with her obvious
looks and large breasts
stuck right under his nose.
She gloated *I'm taken.*

They made him try again
and he chose me.

I saw us blurred around the edges—
projected on a huge screen, the film
unreeling somewhere behind me.
Stars in the black country sky
boiled and hissed till I thought they'd come down
and pulverize me into shining grains.
I had no idea what was happening to me.
I have no idea now

what is happening to me, why
rinsing the lettuce for dinner
as I stare into the fog on the window
can raise me
to the fifth rooftop of wonder, of largeness,
that throws hints in my direction
like earthlight reflected back
from the new moon's almost invisible round.

After the circle dances and goodnight songs
he pressed my hand, then dropped it—
useless to me, a butterfly wing—
and fled.

What am I still getting ready for?

READING THE REFLECTIONS
BACKWARD

Clouds, hills, a clump
of trees. Near them two or three
sheep, reversed in a lake's silver salts—
Change seems suspended, the brakes
are on the universe until
the shining inverted landscape
shivers apart into bright
fragments. A rock is flung, or a prey
dropped mid-flight, and the scene
is once more open to interpretation.
The shore scumbled in an isolate stroke
of mud and gravel, mysterious crease
where reflection and reality meet.
One could go either way.

For this is not concerned wholly
with surfaces, but with the plunge
past the shore's slime, past dragonflies,
lotus stems tangling around the ankles, till
you float out in the sweet depths
of the middle, still enough
to be a part of the reflection,
a speck that suggests to a watcher
that something unobserved
is calling you into existence on the lake—
the artist who puts his portrait on a mirror
in the room he paints, then leaves. You
are the rift in the symmetry. Yet you're

past believing that you would, if you could
penetrate glass, choose the backward world.
Take the sky's blue: it's only
an approximation of light that springs
when you are ready to deliver yourself
to the world, when all you want
is to know that something of yours
has caught. As though you'd spent your life
in a world without mirrors, you must even learn
to recognize your own face, because
to get the reflection right you have to

read it backward: the world
like an etched copper plate the artist,
in a moment of forgetfulness, hastily signed
in the usual way. By hints and whispers
you construct a retrograde landscape,
stepping backward to the line
where the real and reflected worlds converge,
where the silver-backed lake seems
even brighter than air: who would expect
such light to have come out of earth.

PHOTO BY ALISON PORTELLO

Hannah Stein was born in Brooklyn and grew up in upstate New York. Educated at Barnard College and the University of California at Davis, she lives in Davis with her husband, the mathematician Sherman Stein. She has three adult children. Her *Schools of Flying Fish* was published by State Street Press.